KICKBOXING

Joanne Mattern

Rourke

Publishing LLC

Vero Beach, Florida 32964

www.rourkepublishing.com

PHOTO CREDITS: © Alexander Kalina: page 5 top; © Cpl Sarah M. Maynard: page 5 bottom; © Kondrashov Mikail Evgenevich: page 6 right, 9, 15, 17, 19; © Tito Wong: page 6 left; © Pedro Jorge Henriques Monteiro: page 7, 13; © James Church: page 10; © Nicholas Rjabow: page 11; © Sereda Nikolay Ivanovich: page 22

Edited by Kelli L. Hicks

Cover design by Nicola Stratford: bdpublishing.com
Interior design by Renee Brady

Library of Congress Cataloging-in-Publication Data

MatMattern, Joanne, 1963-
 Kickboxing / Joanne Mattern.
     p. cm. -- (Action sports)
 ISBN 978-1-60472-395-3 (Hardcover)
 ISBN 978-1-60472-806-4 (Softcover)
 1. Kickboxing--Juvenile literature. I. Title.
 GV1114.65.M34 2009
 796.815--dc22

                                2008016352

Rourke Publishing

www.rourkepublishing.com – rourke@rourkepublishing.com
Post Office Box 3328. Vero Beach. FL 32964

TABLE OF CONTENTS

WHAT IS KICKBOXING?

Kickboxing is an exciting sport. It is part of a group of sports called the **martial arts**. Kickboxing is a combination of **karate** and **boxing**.

Martial arts started in the Far East. The Far East includes the countries of China, Japan, Korea, and Vietnam. These sports became popular in the United States after World War II (1939-1945). Kickboxing as we know it today started in America in the 1970s.

DID YOU KNOW...

Karate is a Japanese word. It means empty hand. Karate is a kind of fighting that does not use weapons.

A sensei, or martial arts master, leads students through a drill.

These kickboxers are trying to knock each other onto the mat.

Some martial arts use **forms**. People also call these forms **kata**. Forms use a set of traditional movements. The movements in a form are always the same.

Kickboxing is different. There are no forms in kickboxing. Instead, kickboxers move their bodies any way they need to.

Kickboxing is a **full-contact** sport. The athletes hit and kick each other as hard as they can.

KICKBOXING EQUIPMENT

Kickboxers do not use weapons. However, this is a rough sport. Kickboxers must wear **protective** gear to stay safe.

Kickboxers wear foot protectors. These are soft, padded slippers. They keep the athletes from hurting their feet or ankles. Kickboxers also wear shin guards. These thin plastic guards protect the legs from kicks.

Boxing gloves are an important piece of equipment. Gloves protect the hands, fingers, and wrists.

DID YOU KNOW...

At first, kickboxers could not make full contact. People thought it was too dangerous! Finally, people developed safety equipment so athletes could hit and kick without hurting each other.

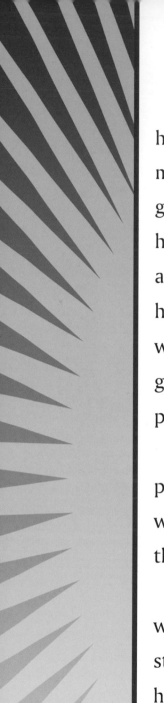

A kickboxer must protect the head and face during a kickboxing match. Kickboxers wear a head guard. A head guard is a soft helmet. It covers the athlete's head and forehead. A thick strap covers his or her neck. Kickboxers also wear a mouth guard. A mouth guard is a piece of rubber that protects the athlete's teeth.

Boys who kickbox wear a cup to protect their **groin**. Girls and boys wear a chest protector under the shirt.

Kickboxers also use thick pads when they practice. These pads let students learn new moves without hurting anyone.

Kickboxers wear helmets and
pads to stay safe during a match.

KICKBOXING PUNCHES AND KICKS

Kickboxers use their hands and feet as weapons. Here are some basic kickboxing moves that use the hands.

The Jab

The jab is the most basic punch. When a person jabs, he or she punches straight at his or her **opponent**.

The Cross

A cross is like a jab, except the kickboxer turns his or her fist as it hits.

The Hook

To do a hook punch, the kickboxer turns his or her hips and shoulders and swings the arm around. This makes the hook a very hard punch!

The Uppercut

An uppercut is a punch straight up to the opponent's chin.

KICKS

There are many ways to use your feet and legs in kickboxing. Here are a few of the most common kicks.

Front Kick

The athlete lifts the foot up and kicks out at the opponent to do a front kick.

Roundhouse Kick

To do this kick, the athlete moves his leg up and around in a half-circle.

Side Kick

In this kick, the athlete kicks to the side and twists the hips.

Back Kick

To do this kick, the athlete kicks straight back and out.

Knee Strikes

The knee can be a powerful weapon. Kickboxers lift their knees to hit an opponent.

DEFENDING YOURSELF

Kickboxing is not just kicking and hitting. A kickboxer must also defend against punches and kicks.

Kickboxers stand in a **defensive stance**. They stand with knees slightly bent. The arms are in front of the body. The fists are in front of the face. This position protects the athlete's groin, stomach, neck, and face.

Kickboxers must always be ready to defend themselves. When a fighter sees a punch or kick coming, he must **block** it. An athlete blocks with the arms, legs, or body.

The kickboxer in the red helmet successfully blocks a kick from his opponent.

BELT RANKINGS

A belt system ranks kickboxers. The color of the belt shows the kickboxers' **rank**. The lowest rank is usually a white or orange belt. The highest rank is a black belt. It can take up to three years of training before an athlete achieves a black belt.

Athletes must pass a test to move up to the next belt color. The test includes physical challenges. The athlete must also show **discipline** and **focus**.

BELT RANKINGS

Every school has its own system of belt colors. Here is a common example:

Orange → Blue → Green → Red → Brown → Black

Belt colors show what rank these kickboxers have achieved. Yellow and blue are usually low to medium ranks.

KICKBOXING STARS

Ernesto Hoost

Ernesto Hoost is a Dutch kickboxer. His nickname is Mr. Perfect. Hoost is a four time world champion. He won his first world championship in 1993. Hoost fought all over the world. He retired in 2006. After he retired, Hoost trained other kickboxers.

Semmy Schilt

Semmy Schilt is the current World Champion. He is the first fighter to win the championship three times in a row! He also holds the record for the longest winning streak.

Bill "Superfoot" Wallace

Bill Wallace won 23 consecutive professional fights between 1974 and 1980. When he retired in 1980, he remained undefeated. Wallace continues to teach the art of kickboxing and has even appeared in movies about the sport.

KICKBOXING COMPETITIONS

Many kickboxers take part in **competitions**. They fight against other kickboxers to see who the best fighter is. Weight classes and skill classes divide kickboxing competitions. Organizers try to match opponents evenly.

Competitions may take place at a martial arts school. They may take place at an arena or a gym. Opponents face each other inside a ring. They wear equipment to protect themselves. A **referee** watches the match, making sure the fight is safe and fair for everyone.

GLOSSARY

block (BLOK): to stop something from hitting you

boxing (BOKS-ing): fighting with your fists

competitions (kom-puh-TIH-shuhnz): a contest

defensive stance (dee-FENS-uhv STANSS): standing with your arms and hands in front of your body to protect yourself

discipline (DISS-uh-plin): control over the way you behave

focus (FOH-kuhss): concentration

forms (FORMZ): a set of traditional movements that are always the same; also called kata

full-contact (FUHL KON-takt): in sports, striking each other very hard

groin (GROYN): the area between the insides of your thighs and your stomach

karate (kuh-RAH-tee): a form of self-defense using kicks and punches

kata (KAH-tah): a set of traditional movements that are always the same; also called forms

kickboxing (KICK-boks-ing): a sport that combines karate and boxing

martial arts (MAR-shuhl ARTZ): a style of fighting from the Far East, such as karate

opponent (uh-POH-nuhnt): a person who is against you in a fight

protective (pruh-TEKT-tihv): something worn to keep you safe

rank (RANK): level or position

referee (ref-uh-REE): a person who supervises a sports match or game

INDEX

WEBSITES TO VISIT

www.americankickboxing.com

www.columbia.edu/cu/kickboxing/history.html

www.kidshealth.org/teen/food_fitness/exercise/kickboxing.html

FURTHER READING

Johnson, Nathan. *Kickboxing*. Mason Crest Publishers, 2003.

Kaelberer, Angie Peterson. *Kickboxing*. Capstone Press, 2006.

Nonnemacher, Klaus. *Kickboxing*. Gareth Stevens Publishing, 2004.

ABOUT THE AUTHOR

Joanne Mattern is the author of more than 300 books for children. She has written about a variety of subjects, including sports, history, animals, and science. She loves bringing nonfiction subjects to life for children! Joanne lives in New York State with her husband, four children, and assorted pets.